"The task of 'the poet' is brilliantly fulfilled with sonics, structure, detail, richness and care. But where this book truly exceeds and excels is in creating a hologram of emotions, a reality we can enter, where aesthetics are crisp and clear enough to create a new paradigm. Poetics that bring emotional worlds into existence have to be held in place with mastery. Someone is obviously in charge of this work. Someone is in control of its precise syntax and beautiful heart. I never wanted to stop reading."

Grace Cavalieri
Henry Morgenthau III Poetry Prize Judge
& author of *The Long Game*

"There is a moment in our life that we know deep within ourselves, yet we ask will it be 'lost or more itself' if we write it down? Only Winifred Hughes asks such questions in her breathtakingly expansive yet focused book. Stand by the water, ask 'What does the water remember / as it slides in and out of itself'? She suggests an answer, not the answer, but one along with others that you will not be able to shake off."

David Sten Herrstrom

Author of *Light as Experience and Imagination from Paleolithic to Roman Times*

"In Hughes' work we enter into a stunning linguistic and emotional landscape of give and take, of push and pull, each step forward a constant realignment of understanding of nature and history, of temporality itself. 'How can I lose what has not been?' Hughes writes. And 'Will I simply step out of / chronology?' *The Village of New Ghosts* moves brilliantly by way of questioning. There is a hesitation, a shifting back and forth between the known and the unknowable, what can be reached and that which one, despite all odds, continues moving towards. Everything 'still so familiar, yet so estranged.'"

EJ Colen
Author of *What Weaponry* and *The Green Condition*

the village *of* new ghosts

Cover art: Christine Drawl
First Edition 2024
Published in the United States of America
Printed by Spencer Printing
ISBN 978-1-7355148-8-8

Publisher's Cataloging-in-Publication
(Provided by Cassidy Cataloguing Services, Inc.)

Names: Hughes, Winifred, 1948- author.
Title: The village of new ghosts / Winifred Hughes.
Description: First edition. | Baltimore, MD : Passager Books, 2024.
Identifiers: ISBN: 978-1-7355148-8-8
Subjects: LCSH: Loss (Psychology)--Poetry. | Widowhood--Poetry. | Families--Poetry. | Spirituality-- Poetry. | Change--Poetry. | Nature--Poetry. | Dyslexia--Poetry. | China--History--Poetry. | LCGFT: Poetry. | BISAC: POETRY / General. | POETRY / Subjects & Themes / Death, Grief, Loss. | POETRY / Women Authors.
Classification: LCC: PS3608.U376 V55 2024 | DDC: 811/.6--DC23

Passager Books
7401 Park Heights Avenue
Baltimore, Maryland 21208
www.passagerbooks.com

the village *of* new ghosts

Winifred Hughes

Passager Books
Baltimore, MD
2024

CONTENTS

II

to Adam and Alex
in memory of Fred

In the Village of New Ghosts

MENG CHIAO

Have you lost your way there, so new
and unfamiliar without me?
Does it have streets and houses?
Are there streetlights or is light forbidden?
Are you lonely or is it overcrowded?
Is it strange to you as this place
is to me—the lanes we walked together
not really noticing how narrow they were,
how they blurred into a maze,
or how many doors there were to open
with nothing behind them,
buildings with nothing inside.
I walk them now in a sort of daze, astonished
to discover the present amid the past,

seasons blurring into one long seasonless tunnel,

twilight indistinct, though nothing much has changed.

Sometimes I feel superimposed on someplace else,
  exactly the same.

Sometimes I hear footsteps, hesitant as mine.

Will you follow at whatever distance

if I don't look back?

I

Swimming Lesson

In the shallow end
of the blue pool, I am learning

how to breathe, after years
of suffocating and not

knowing it. I am becoming
reacquainted with the air

as I abandon it,
slip back into a time

when someone else breathed
for me and into me,

breathed form into water
and unfitted it for

water, left me stranded
in the sting of air.

Juggling

Nothing stabilizes: the brain imprints
movement shape. Each toss

arcs slightly higher, lower,
a fraction sideways,

each an infinitesimal mistake,
the trick not to catch it, fix it,

but keep it moving, bend into
elliptical orbit the recurring

balls, rings, teacups, tennis racquets
or flaming torches that take off

and come to hand. What jugglers
learn: not pattern or precision

but ways to compensate, to drop
and still recover. A kind of

natural selection: each move
or generation improvised.

What jugglers practice
is letting fall.

Momentarily

If it goes unrecorded, will the moment be
lost or more itself? Will it slip through

the interstices, fade into the next as it
absorbed the one before? Just a moment—

will it be longer or shorter, will we be in it
or oblivious, will it still unite us in time

if not in place or in temper, will it last
exactly for a moment and no more

but equally no less? Is it in this spill
of sunlight over newly green willows,

in the glance of water over stones? In this one
afternoon of nothing more? Of such stillness

melting into itself and into itself until we can't
tell but think maybe, and then it is gone.

Painting from Memory

When he was old, his vision
occluded, Monet kept on painting
from memory: from the feel

of the brush in his hand, cross
grain of the canvas, worn labels
on the tubes of pigment:

an old man remembering
the look of water caught
under bridges, the shafts

and poolings of light, rough edges
expanding into water and light:
his strokes bolder, a little

defiant, the world turned brash
orange and brown, antithetical
blue: the blurring of time

and detail an almost
forgetting. Did he keep on
loving from memory:

old gestures reclaimed, longing
unchanged, heart's pigments
spilling and pooled?

Dyslexic

Eye won't track
the pencil in the doctor's
hand or on the spread page.
Look where d is tumbling into p,
f and g bait each other
with barbed hooks, look
what means the same
right to left, slantwise, upside
down. How did sounds get
flattened, round world into
black scratches, jugglers'
dropped oranges and apples
still spinning on the blank
sheet, all the pith
pounded out of them,
eye stammering for something
real to look at, hand no
thing to grip. Words dance.
Sith this pot is top, but may
be tub. Toom is moot.
We might not die as
palindrome. So call it
spelling, cast that spell
on the misspoken
ones, some of us born
that way, some
headed there.

Up-Island Everyone Spoke Sign

CHILMARK, MARTHA'S VINEYARD

Soundless, their words became tactile,
shaped in the hands. They thought

little of it, so many deaf on the island,
the hearing ones bilingual, signing

instinctively, function or eloquence
at their fingertips, on the tips of tongues.

And the deaf were just that, deaf, as
they might have been short or raven-

haired. No one saw anything amiss.
Farmers, fishermen, shipwrights,

shopkeepers, they knew their customers.
Deaf and hearing intermarried, speech

palpable between them, deftly knitting
the silence, its invisible strands.

Depth of Field

VICTORIAN PORTRAITS

Could we keep it up
as they did, five or ten
minutes at a stretch,

poised and exposed
before the slowed shutter
shuts us down?

A sigh, absentminded
shift or blink, and the image
blurs successive

selves together. Could we
gaze at time's measured
passage without a flinch,

look truth right back at it,
our characters deepening
visibly as we sit

waiting for nothing more
than to stop the wait—
mouth taut, eyes remote

or anguished, a presence
surfacing we hadn't known
inside us.

Architecture Student

Given latitude and map,
          she fixes Venice
for her site plan,

conjures up a floating
          opera house
mid-canal—anchorless,

flung against no sky,
          its matchbox chambers
measuring a spatial music.

The professor wants a "story,"
          persuasiveness
of line, meta-geometry

not lived-in storeys,
          cracked plaster,
gutters and plumbing.

It doesn't have to hold
          water, just hover
over the mind's grid.

You have to learn, he says,
          how to play, how
not to fasten things

with bolts and mortar,
          design no place to be
but to imagine being.

Color, Pigments

How to measure blackness
in its exact degrees (*lampblack*,

ink black, *anthracite*,
aniline)—that is an art

not inculcated in life
drawing, choose among

the crimped tubes of *drop black*,
bone black, *direct deep black*,

the double-dyed, the blacker.
It wouldn't come

from well-rinsed brushes,
spit-and-polished leather,

but pasted labels in the blacking
factory, Victorian child

clad in deep mourning.
Black should be

immedial—no compromise,
no seed for planting

in this blackened soil,
the stain *ungreenable black*.

In Lieu of Elegy

A word that was not spoken
Seems to deepen silence.
How can I lose what has not been?

A child that was not born
Needs no voice.
She leaves her words unspoken.

The stairs unclimbed, the steps not worn
In what never was her house.
She cannot find what has not been

Though she inhabits its thin
Element. She does not miss
Her bed unwarmed, my word not spoken,

Her life not lived in.
Only I can feel her resonance.
She does not know what has not been.

She does not take my hand. Then
I am brought to silence.
I know our words will not be spoken
And I have lost what has not been.

Following

behind me, when I walk,
        a human figure, fully
spatial, dimensional, close
        on my heels, grazing
my shoulders, turning when
        I turn, backing up
whenever I back into it:
        a solid self, but
whose? or when I sit,
        enfolding me in my own
arms, or whose arms?
        wedged against the back
of the chair: a stalker, duplicate,
        conjoined twin, birth
mother? someone I missed or
        just recently found:
a tweak of the *angular gyrus*,
        the body's felt sensation
of hovering, looking down on
        itself, on myself,
from above: then who is looking,
        who is feeling, is the body
a sensation of the brain,
        how many bodies am I
inhabiting, am I running away from,
        which of us is duped?

Cornelian: Keats in Italy

An oval stone: the shape
of what is cool and smooth
in the fevered palm. A tool

to soothe the seamstress's cramped
fingers, stitchers of mourning
garments, pillow slips for the long

sleep of the newly dead. A touch
beyond touch of the insensible,
of the undying, on the dying flesh:

as much as he could bear
of love, of longing, a lingering
thought of her, a last sensation;

hard, unyielding fragment
of earth's stubbornness, but worn
by handling, till he could not let go.

At the Jetties

Stone chimneys loosely piled
above the dunes—all that remains

of a phantom house, and I think,
this is the past, what it looks like

now. I think, *I have lived*
in this house. I've tasted

the salt air, looked out through
exactly this angle of light

onto this grey sea, I remember
the shape of the waves, that's what

memory is, the shape of waves,
and when the waves recede

strange shapes of driftwood, sea
wrack, sea glass, grey smoke

wavering from stone chimneys,
after flames had engulfed the house.

After the Storm

I see you as I might have remembered you,
stopped short in this momentary skin.

I see myself turned away, both of us enclosed
in a museum's glassed-in case. How long

have we lived this half-forgotten scene, the air
like fallen leaves around us, a sunset under foot?

Light is a sepia wash: my face is tinged with it,
the past already in my mouth.

Fire

When the house finally caught fire,
wood frame collapsing
into the wood-burning stove,

she stumbled out with the others
into a chill November night.
One child still missing

and she went back in
though she found no doorway
and no child.

The others waited.
She returned
a woman made of flame.

They took her back
among them, but she could not
again be flesh.

Meditations of an Old Woman

I am a stranger
in this house. Where else
have I been living
these fifty years? I hold
a key in one hand,
walk down bare corridors,
I lose my way
in uninhabited rooms.

I am a stranger
in this body. It has
a strange smell.
It wants other things.
I forget to feed it
so it eats secretly.
It hides things from me,
it can't be trusted.

I am a stranger
in this dying. I open
the wrong doors. I don't
know where to put things.
The latches have come
unfastened, clocks have
forgotten where to point.
There is someone else
in the mirror.

Distances

How many light years is it
to where the light still shines
from the windows of your father's house,
the bulb of the goose-necked lamp
stretched out over his papers
as he scrawls away darkness
till three in the morning,
the fluorescent coil in the kitchen
radiant over your mother's bent head,
her chapped hands still scrubbing the dishes,
the nightlight under the doorframe
as you sleep with your brothers and sister,
dreaming, unknowing?

Family Portrait as the Brontës

Branwell painted it—himself and three
sisters crowded together, Charlotte
foursquare and stoical, Emily remote,
Anne looking up, her head slightly bowed.
Dissatisfied, he blotted himself out, leaving
the remains of his shirt collar and a vaporous
column of pale yellow pigment enveloping
the shadow of his face and hair, so that he is
not there yet still an undeniable presence.
As children, they had been inseparable, bound
by Gondal and Angria, the harrowing sagas
of their avatars. Soon they would all be gone.

When I look at us now—the stacks of old
photographs of the four of us—children
peering out of a more and more distant
childhood, squinting in the long-ago sun,
I remember fragments of our own tales
acted out in costume. I remember our
alternate names. I see one of us blurred,
painted out, his childish face slowly
dissolving, the rest of us still unaware.

Meng Chiao Mourns Lu Yin

Reading Meng Chiao's lament for his friend
so soon after your death, I am falling

through a dozen centuries into
an autumn night like this one, wind

restless as a burial song, scattered
rain and spent leaves, moon blotted out.

Which autumn is it? It is the same
lament: *this one grief*, he says,

blurs us and the ancients together
as the times collapse, mine into his,

his into time beyond time, yours
into dust. I too have looked into

a face white as old jade,
unrecognizable yet deeply,

undeniably known, a face
unreadable now as it was then.

"Kingfishers Catch Fire"

G. M. HOPKINS

She lifts her wrists reverently, holds them out
before her, skin paper-thin, falling away
into infinite creases; hands loosely clenched,
one still swollen from stroke. She looks at them
as though they could not be hers, they must
belong somewhere else. She looks at me, eyes
flat, irises appearing crushed, leaking unevenly
at the edges, yet still a bright blue-green.
She says, *What shall I do with these bones?*
as though I must know the answer.

She sits in the wheelchair, folding in on herself.
Her eyes study me, and fall. Her lips part. The sounds
are not quite articulate. Do you remember? I say.
And she tells me how she used to walk to school
ninety years ago in Birmingham, who used
to live in the houses she passed. I show her
a picture and she makes a face, like a schoolgirl.
Miss Brew (headmistress, 1923). *But she was*
fatter than that. One day I wear a grey wool sweater.
That was my mother's, she says, *she gave it to you*.
She does not say how her mother died, engulfed
in flame. How the house burned down.

On Tuesdays, Kim brings the Eucharist: Body
of Christ. She chews and swallows, one hand
signing a broken cross. This is my body:

what shall I do with it? *My father lived there,*
she says, *that door across the road. Don't*
open it. I tell her about the kingfisher hovering
above the pond this morning. *What was that poem?*
she asks. I read it: "As kingfishers catch fire . . . ."
For a moment her eyes ignite. "What I do is me:
for that I came." For this? we have all come,
"Each mortal thing." She lies in the hospital bed,
the lift hulking along the side like a gibbet.
She tells me something, over and over.
Oh, I don't know what I'm saying.

Prologue

My grandmother died before I was born.
She lived in parts of two centuries
long before this one, in places where
I have mostly never been. She was
beautiful, I know; she was greatly loved.
On the day before she left England, she wore
a cloche hat and low-waisted wool coat
for the family portrait. It was 1923.
I have nothing of hers, just the photograph
and a few stray pieces of silverware.
Everything else was lost in the fire.

Where is she now—a memory of a memory,
my faulty recollection of the stories
my mother told and I half-listened to.
I imagine her a girl in Birmingham, one
of ten siblings, dressed in costume to play
Shakespeare, snuggled together under the covers
at night to make their own central heating.
No one is left who touched her.

My Mother's Oranges

A little girl in England after the war
ate twenty-seven small oranges

from a wooden crate that had
found its way to her parents' door

amid the loss and the aftermath.
After the years of drinking blue milk,

and no butter, she couldn't stop eating
until she was sick, couldn't stop tearing

the bittersweet fruit that the animal
inside her instinctively devoured.

Some Presence

So far away under ground
lost to yourself
still you find my place
of dreaming and enter it
unwilling to let go
as of breath when you hardly
could draw it but kept on
gasping for some
habitable element,
some fragment when nothing
could be whole, some presence
unreasonably persisting
even in someone else's dream

In Early March

I missed her dying.

How could I not have been there
after so many days of watching

at her bedside, reading poem
after poem as though words

could have something to do
with this shutting down, as though

silence needed words to contain it,
as though words might be breath?

Someone else heard the last, someone
else touched his hand to her eyes,

while I had gone from the books
that she loved into the raw poem

of the marsh at dusk in the last
of winter to see the clumps of reeds

dissolving into mist, the slice of sky
holding out against encroaching

extinction, and the small bodies
of woodcocks launching themselves

into that lowering remnant of sky.

II

"I Inhabit My Absence"

TU FU

So much keener than presence,
more spacious—I have not

plumbed all its shadowy depths
nor climbed its remoter peaks.

No wind in the leaf-lorn boughs,
no voice calling my other name.

Houseboat anchorless, adrift,
my only lantern a new moon.

Inhabit? —I haunt it, wear out
the rough-hewn planks, midnight

pacing—it is the only place
where I might have found you.

A Bird-While

EMERSON'S JOURNALS

As long as a bird will hold still, will tolerate
human presence, let us in on the secret

it embodies but cannot impart, allow us
a glimpse of its crest, the pattern on its throat,

flick of its tail, wing bars, snatch of song
before it escapes our space, our notions

of temporal sequence—that is a "bird-while."
Just long enough, or not quite, but not a bit

longer. Emerson thought it was so familiar,
so much the same—that breathless interval,

pause in the rhythm of flitting—it might serve
as a unit of time for a "natural chronometer."

Do you remember that fall when a chickadee
came for the seed in your hand and alighted,

feather to flesh, a small scratching of claws,
and everything stopped, for a bird-while?

Walking

When we set out on pilgrimage
we followed all the footsteps

from before, Neolithic pathways,
deer tracks, portages, dry streambeds,

ridges worn down into hollows,
mule trails edging into canyons.

We thought we were walking the brink
of the world, thin line the sky draws

around itself—walking circles, cycles,
map into mind, footsore passages

of distance into time, each milepost
a function of duration, cairns loosely

piled as provisional waymarks,
not boundaries or ends.

Streamwatch

What does the water remember
as it slides in and out of itself

moment by moment exchanging
itself for itself, each molecule

at once unique and the same
bearing traces of solute only

detectable by targeted reagents
turning to murky purples or greens

in a test tube held up to the light?
What reagent will precipitate

our history—laughter, picnics, vows sworn
along the banks, laments keyed

to the murmur of waters over stone?
What else is the water saying,

unique and the same over centuries
of babbling to itself, fading

downstream and starting up again
still trying to get it right?

Imprinted

I might have forgotten that moment
when the sunlight fell into silence
along the sand at Vineyard Sound,

opened a chink in the long afternoon
letting in light that imprinted
water and sand, white egret

poised at the verge, still
as forgetting or absence,
scallop hard-edged in my hand,

trailing seaweed rooted
to the vacant shell. The touch
we felt and withheld.

Low Tide, Katama

The water withdraws
                    in runlets
          wavering to the sea,
                    peels back
          to expose bare skin
                              underneath:

the mudflats black, traced with
                    long lines
          of knotted algae,
                    bloated jellies,

egg sacks, shards of abandoned
                    clam shells—
          angelwings, razors, scallops—
                              the cast
          paper-thin shapes
                    of horseshoe crabs,

and the mixed flocks of shorebirds
          that straggle in,
                    dredging and dredging,
                              ingesting
                    the raw life forms:

black mud all that is, germ of
all that will be,
remains
of all that once was:
open just now,
soon to be overrun: I will
search
for it, nothing but

brackish water over my ankles,
no traces
of what was teeming before,
no such place
on the ground,
only the map
inside my head.

Brooking

Brook keeps rushing by
fluent uncontained
rock-rinsing
oxygen-dissolving

we peer in tipsy with motion
not ours
pulse beating
off-balance

we reflect
spacetime
down there

its shallow rill
holds everything:

tree trunks kneeling
at the brink
bowed branches
water striders' shadows

whole receding depths of sky
of time

the past rushing past
tumbling over
unsettled future
our past? together?
everything garbled

in water-speak
what we said
our bodies rippling
unsteady voices

Static

Static left from seconds after
the big bang still floating around
the selvages of the universe

if only you can hear deep
enough, probe far enough
into spacetime, let your body

absorb the waves of vibration
tuned before time could
gather itself into moments

or eons—timelessness still
hanging around at the fringes
of time, beginnings still defying

its passage. What we said
to each other not yet unsaid,
our words still resonating

somewhere beyond us and after
us, if only I could listen far
enough away.

Timepiece

If I put on your watchband
so it touches where it touched
the tender place on the underside

of your wrist, if I buckle it,
will I feel your pulse still
surging, will I relive your time,

each second replayed as it
once was, or will it just stop?
Will I simply step out of

chronology? Or your sweater,
if I wear it, will it displace
me or wrap me in its arms?

If I sleep on your pillow,
will I dream of you or dream
your old dreams?

The Scene Without

"The scene" is still the same—that's what you called it,
the view from our back windows that opens in winter

like a spread scroll—the brook that runs free and full,
skidding
among stones, browned meadows with their broken stems

and grasses, matted leafmold, woods stripped of cover
spilling pent up secrets, light pallid, whether bleak or tender

only you could have told. You'd still know it instantly—
how you
loved the scope of it, the sheer expanse; loved even the
battered,

colorless stalks, the twiggy bushes, hollow seedpods—
remnants
of your care only last summer, no longer ago than that, now

unbridgeable by any quickening of spring, unimaginable
by any
thought of mine. Only this morning I saw a sharp-shinned
hawk

gliding overhead, ready to plunge. Before that a fox, uttering
its short, sharp yap, then loping across the yard to re-enact

the primal plot that ends in survival and abrupt extinction.
Small songbirds enact it too, gorging against the cold but not

to the point of slowing their flight from the hawk.
   Look there—
I want to show you the brown creeper camouflaged against

the mottled bark, until it spirals down to the base of the
   trunk;
the golden-crowned kinglet flitting skittishly among the
   bare

branches, picking at lichens; the flicker, with its yellow-
   shafted wings
and dagger-like bill, drilling for grubs in the half-thawed
   ground.

I wonder if they might be the same individual birds you saw
   this time
last year, looking out from these same windows on this
   winter scene.

I want to tell you that they are all still here, that I am still here,
   that nothing
has changed—just everything inside the windows, but
   nothing without.

July

Late July: time unravels.

Was it exactly a year ago
that it was late July?

Time blanked, leached
by this monotonous sun,

hammered flat as scorched grass.
Cicadas' dry, monotonous drone

the last sound you heard before
thought was extinguished, time

scattered into irrecoverable
fragments. I need no grammar

for the cicadas' language,
indistinct as time's passage,

the markers removed or erased.

Revenant

I held back one key, which let me in
where I have no rights now but had
for so many years—let me in to that
particular past, not just the long ago,

though that too, but the rawly recent,
as close to now as your drawn breath,
the past we lived in in this house
only months ago, as we always had,

as though it would go on as it always
had, as though we could own it as we
owned these timbers and shingles,
these windows to look out on the bay

and the ocean, these doors to shut us in.
And now I have sold them, as though I
could sell the past, which is our only
place now, the only house that is not

just mine but ours, sold it as though
other people could own it—our house,
our past—as though they could simply
move in and move on, the house itself

mute and helpless, piled up with all
the incidentals of going out and going in—
beach equipment, cheery maritime prints
and hangings, braided rugs, wicker furniture,

now detritus I am sorting through for more
keys to what's irrevocably locked, where
I can enter only obliquely, only alone. I walk
the rooms, still so familiar, yet so estranged.

I'm not supposed to be here, I'm as ghostly
as you are, but seeing and feeling, alive
in what's invisible, what's meaningless
to anyone else, now even to you. Can I

reach you here, you then but here,
if nowhere else—simply open a door
and walk into what's gone? Out front
the buyers have heaped up what they don't

want—chipped crockery, a glass tabletop,
heavy wooden wardrobe broken into rough
planks, the drawers handleless and gaping
that once held fragments of our daily living,

that we could pull open and find something
we were looking for, something we could grasp
and take for granted, now emptied out like
our time together as tenants of this house.

Tako-Tsubo: Broken-Heart Syndrome

The heart has become a trap:
engorged to the shape
of an octopus-pot, *tako-tsubo*,
it baits and snaps shut.

Take my heart on a trawler
out of Menemsha,
throw it overboard and see
what it will catch.

In the Chinese Library

I'm illiterate in your library,
books unreadable, bristling
with thickets of print—
arrows sharpened pointedly

showing where I can't follow,
antic characters waving
their arms, letting down ladders
on the bindings, scampering

backwards down them,
leading me to the bottom
of some crucial enigma
or insight, or is it merely astray?

I'll never know now, you
can't tell me, can't decipher
what eludes me, here
or elsewhere, as you used

to do. I drove you crazy
asking the unanswerable
and you would try, quite
seriously, until you broke

down in exasperation
or laughter. How I loved you
for trying. You never quit
studying Mandarin, devouring

whole dictionaries, cover
to cover, however
indigestible that might seem.
You never stopped wanting

to know, though it took you
a lifetime. I want to trace
your footsteps on my own
but these ideographs

have become nothing
more than rows of empty
constructs, untranslatable
to me except as you.

Forecast

Featureless weather: the sky has drawn a blank,
forgotten shape and color, what happened

long ago or only this morning. We have no
mnemonic for clouds, no sketch of a lopsided

circle with stiff rays sticking out around it.
Will we forget what we once meant to do,

what could be said? What other memories—
loss of a key, long ride in a rickety boat,

your touch—will the sky obliterate?
Rain would be a relief.

Wasque Point

Sometimes a place washes over me
in relentless riptide, its spit

of sand a frail barrier against
a whole ocean's immensity,

flocks of late-summer shore birds
ebbing and flowing with the waves,

sun-flashes off them, the light
rebounding upwards, the scene

twice-lit, re-illuminated from below.
I can taste the salt breeze,

feel it shivering over sun-warmed
skin, and there you are again

casting and casting your fishing line
into uncertain currents, not

particularly expecting to catch a fish,
sometimes catching one anyway

as I keep on casting into oceans of time
to catch a glimpse of this place.

Thought

For a time the world
thought you, burned

through you, as you
thought the world

into *now*, right *now*, this
moment, your singular

grasp of it: leafbud,
cloudburst, turbid stream

spilling over mudbanks,
your own skin inter-

face with the world,
still holding you in

until the world forgot
and you stopped thinking

it, stopped thinking yourself,
and the banks overflowed,

the world no longer wide
enough to contain you.

Dreamer

Did we dream each other all

those years a long sleep, double sleep

inventing new selves, or did we each

wander unwitting into the same

dream dreamt by someone else, deep

sleeper, steady breather breathing us,

another subconscious merging ours,

seamless sleeping broken

by sudden apnea, one intermittently

wakened, the other now dreamless

sleeper in my dream.

Your Ring

A safe place—where I meant
          to put it, where I thought

I had—so safe that it can't be
          recovered even by loving

so long, so hard. I keep looking
          in wrong places—where

would you have put it I wonder,
          but you never took it off

until they gave it to me in the ER
          with the contents of your pockets

and I brought it home and lost
          it. I suppose it's somewhere,

I suppose everything has to be
          somewhere even if it's lost.

Houseplants

I keep watering the houseplants whether they want it
  or not.

You never let me near them.

Though once long ago, when you hardly knew me,
  you asked me

to look after your spectacular coleus for a week.

I held my breath till you returned.

One summer the renters watered the artificial hydrangea.

I probably would have done the same.

Now the houseplants miss you, even if I talk to them.

So far three of them have died.

But not the hanging spider plant you brought home
  thirty-five years ago

in a small plastic pot it has since outgrown.

Garden Without a Gardener

You planted nothing this year and it came up
along with a riotous crop of everything you didn't

plant, you didn't pull out and pile up for compost
—pale weedy shoots and grasses, nameless

and opportunistic, repeating themselves over
and over, poking between perennials, spreading

monotonously over barren patches, vigorous
with unwanted and superfluous life. Even last

summer you toiled against the odds, attempting
to impose your idea of order. You turned the earth,

you set herbs—thyme, oregano, basil. One day
in August I harvested twenty jalapeños, I tried

to tell you but you were hearing something else
or maybe nothing at all. How quickly the garden

has reverted, become no longer a garden, but not
re-wilding either, some hybrid of intentional

and purposeless that seems to mirror my internal
state. I feel defenseless against it, don't know how

to revive it—the garden was so much yours—
but I can't bear to let it go.

Water Shadows

We throw our shadows down
          downward into moving water

as the water throws its shadows up
          upside down like wind wavering

along the overhanging leaves and branches:
          our shadows drowned, unsteady

in their unfamiliar element but not
          surfacing any time soon, not

coming back to us, pieces of ourselves
          cast away or set free

while the water entangles our world
          in its insubstantial net.

In Mem.

How long is memory?

Does it open and shut,

expand and contract?

Will it outlast us?

Is it graven on tombstones

or sparked in synapses?

Is it a fleeting glimpse,

a glance between us

with everything in it

that no one else knew,

wordless when you had lost

your words?

Is it a place

I can still visit

and not be alone?

How much have I already

unremembered?

Confusing Fall

Equinoctial winds blowing migrant birds
        from the north
tropical gales with exotic names
           from the south,
    balancing act of daylight
           and dark:
we don't know whether to loll with
        lingering summer
    or clench ourselves
           against the cold:
will the wind blow away our preconceptions?
    How to sort out our gusting
        emotions, the past
    piling up like desiccated leaves:
that long fall when someone was dying
    slowly and it was you and I
        couldn't believe it was
           happening as the days
    began to ripen and curdle,
           mingling
        fruition with decay.

◆

Taking refuge in the field guide, its promise
        of certainty, arrows
           pointing to

definitive field marks, only
to find two pages
at the back
labeled “confusing fall warblers”:
small birds, immature
or molting,
trying not to look like themselves
but to blend in
with mixed flocks
of migrants
heading south for their lives.
In the field they’re hard to distinguish,
flitting
manically, voiceless without
their songs of spring.

◆

Even proverbial
in the bander’s hand
half an ounce of feathers,
of bounding heartbeat
and hollow bones,
a flycatcher,
genus *Empidonax*:
but which of several species?
Is the plumage
more greenish
or greyish? Is that
a tinge of yellow
across the breast?

"Oh well—we'll never know,"
the bander says with a shrug
slackening her fingers
as the bird wrenches away.

◆

Misshapen moon—
a lopsided
waning gibbous sulking
in its misty hood
crossed by
millions of silhouettes
of migrating passerines
propelled
by desire
and nocturnal tailwinds
some of them recent fledglings
headed back
to where they've never been
instinctively, unerringly
tuned in
to earth's magnetic field.

◆

Day after day of rain,
woods sodden,
clouds blurred, horizon
smudged,

pressure of the atmosphere around us
unsettled, unsettling:
we've lost all sense of place
or time,
seasons indistinct,
nondescript as confused warblers
dropping from the sky
famished, eyes shut against exhaustion.

◆

Slogging through marsh and upland,
stumbling around in my life,
I keep forgetting
appointments
which I've neglected to inscribe
on rocks or treebark
or in the shifting strands
of cirrus
scribbled across autumn sky.
When I check the cell it proclaims
"No upcoming events,"
the future a blank
like the screen
as time falls backwards
down invisible stairs.

By the Brook

It was the sound of water, a small
gurgling and rushing overheard

in darkness that first entranced us,
sound in motion, motion in sound

that drew us back and we never left
but entered this house as a hermit crab

enters its shell and becomes a part
of it, part of each other and of these walls,

concrete block and wood, by the side
of water passing through on its way

unstoppable as the years that kept
rushing us past.

Album

Time pressed like a picked flower

dried and flattened to a stain of itself.

Is it dross or essence?

On one page you are fishing again.

On another you are a child with a fishing pole.

On the next a father teaching his sons to fish.

You are wearing the t-shirt they would later cut off you.

On one page we are together again holding hands

on the Great Wall or eloping to family court.

I used to want to live the moment in the moment.

You wanted to preserve it on film but you didn't

want to pick flowers: murder to collect.

There are still blank pages where I can paste in your absence.

I can warp time just by flipping through.

Let's live it all again.

Whose hand will turn these pages in a hundred years?

AUTHOR'S NOTES

The Village of New Ghosts:

In his poem "Mourning Lu Yin," Meng Chiao alludes to the Chinese tradition of a place in the afterlife for the newly dead. I found the idea of "new" ghosts, not yet used to being no longer alive, profoundly moving and wanted to imagine what their experience would be like.

"In the Village of New Ghosts" (p. *i*):

Meng Chiao (751-814) was a minor civil servant and conventional poet until late in life, when he began writing long experimental sequences, dark in tone, that confirmed his status as a major figure of T'ang poetry and heir of Tu Fu. The first volume of his poems in English, *The Late Poems of Meng Chiao* translated by David Hinton, appeared only in 1996.

"Up-Island Everyone Spoke Sign" (p. 6):

I spent parts of thirty summers with my family on Martha's Vineyard, where I learned the story of the large deaf population up-island from the mid-seventeenth century to the mid-twentieth. The condition was caused by a recessive gene carried by settlers from England who remained isolated and inbred on the island. It was notable that there was no stigma or discrimination associated with being deaf.

"Architecture Student" (p. 8):

The scale model of an opera house in Venice was an architecture school project of a friend's daughter.

"Meng Chiao Mourns Lu Yin" (p. 20):

The quoted phrases are from David Hinton's translation of "Mourning Lu Yin."

"'I Inhabit My Absence'" (p. 31):

The title is from David Hinton's translation of "Night" by Tu Fu (712-770), long considered the greatest poet of the T'ang period in China.

ACKNOWLEDGMENTS

Atlanta Review
"Up-Island Everyone Spoke Sign," "*Tako-Tsubo:* Broken-Heart Syndrome" (contest honorable mention)

Decodings: Society for Literature and Science Newsletter
"Juggling"

Fish Anthology 2023
"The Scene Without" (overall winner)

The Formalist
"In Lieu of Elegy"

Frost Flowers (Finishing Line Press 2019)
"At the Jetties," "Momentarily"

Larcom Review
"Swimming Lesson"

Nine-Bend Bridge (Red Berry Editions 2015)
"'I Inhabit My Absence'"

Passager

"Imprinted" (contest honorable mention)

Poetry

"Dyslexic," "Depth of Field"

Robinson Jeffers Tor House Poetry Prize

"Revenant" (honorable mention)

Silk Road

"Architecture Student"

U.S. 1 Worksheets

"Fire," "Distances," "My Mother's Oranges"

Wild Leaf Press

"'Kingfishers Catch Fire'" (contest winner)

FURTHER ACKNOWLEDGMENTS

Special thanks go to my sister Hildred Crill and to the regulars at the long poems gatherings—Emily Nguyen, Frederick Tibbitts, David Sten Herrstrom, Lois Marie Harrod, Barbara Williams, and Judith McNally. Members of the Princeton Research Forum poetry group have provided endless fellowship and support.

PHOTO BY ALEX SPAR

Winifred (Winnie) Hughes is a reformed academic and active birder living in Princeton, NJ. Winnie comes from a "whole family of scribblers": her mother Josephine Nicholls Hughes was a poet, her father Riley Hughes, a novelist, and her three siblings, all writers, including her sister Hildred Crill, a poet who lives in Stockholm. Currently she teaches nature writing and ecopoetry at the Watershed Institute in Pennington, NJ, and leads many bird walks in the local open spaces. She is author of two prize-winning chapbooks, *Frost Flowers* (2019) and *Nine-Bend Bridge* (2015). *The Village of New Ghosts* is her first full-length collection of poetry.

Winnie is a longtime member of U.S. 1 Poets Cooperative, established in the 70s, dedicated to fostering new poets. She was married to the late Fred Spar; their two grown sons are Adam and Alex Spar.

The Henry Morgenthau III First Book Poetry Prize was established in 2018 by the Morgenthau children to honor their late father Henry Morgenthau III, who began writing poetry in his 90s. Passager published his first book of poems, *A Sunday in Purgatory*, when Henry was 99. As he said, *To finally, in my nineties, be able to write and publish poems—to connect with other people from my deepest, truest self—was a gift. To be open to others in this way . . . I don't know why I waited so long.*

The prize is awarded every other year to a U.S. poet 70 or older who has not published a full-length book of poetry and furthers Passager's mission to make public the extraordinary work of older writers. The 2024 winner of the Morgenthau Prize is Winifred Hughes for her book *The Village of New Ghosts.*

Past Winners:

Mark Elber, *Headstone*, 2022
Dennis H. Lee, *Tidal Wave*, 2020

for more information about the prize, visit our website at *www.passagerbooks.com*

In legends, the crane stands for longevity, peace, harmony, good fortune and fidelity. A high flyer, it is cherished for its ability to see both heaven and earth. These ancient, magnificent birds, so crucial in the wild as an "umbrella species," are now endangered and must be protected.

Passager Books is dedicated to making public the passions of a generation vital to our survival.

If you would like to support Passager Books, please visit our website www.passagerbooks.com or email us at editors@passagerbooks.com.

The Village of New Ghosts was designed and typeset by Christine Drawl. The pages are set in Garamond Premier Pro and Mrs. Eaves.

The cover art is a painting by Christine Drawl, created using charcoal dust, water and india ink.

Printed in 2024 by Spencer Printing in Honesdale, PA.

ALSO FROM PASSAGER BOOKS

Plain Sight
poems by DAVID BERGMAN

Mothernest
poems by SANDY LONGLEY

The Solitude of Memory
poems by MICHAEL MILLER

Grandfather's Mandolin
poems by FRAN MARKOVER

Ox Horn Bend
a memoir by ROY CHENG TSUNG

Prayers of Little Consequence
poems by GILBERT ARZOLA

For the complete list, visit passagerbooks.com